Sam's
Supersonic
Hamster

Adam and Charlotte Guillain

Illustrated by Andrés Martínez Ricci

OXFORD
UNIVERSITY PRESS

Chapter 1

Sam and his supersonic hamster

Sam was just an ordinary kid. He loved football. He hated cabbage. He had a supersonic pet hamster called Hercules.

HANG ON! A supersonic hamster?

Yes! Hercules was a hamster superhero.

He saved a cat from a fire.

He saved a baby in a runaway pushchair.

He even saved Sam from being late
for tea!

Hercules was the perfect
supersonic hamster ...

... most of the time.

Chapter 2

Fudge river rescue

One morning, Sam was walking to school. He saw a crowd of kids outside the fudge factory. They were staring at something. It looked like an alien spaceship!

'That's strange,' muttered Sam. 'Wake up, Hercules!' But Hercules just snored.

The factory roof blew off and thick
oozy fudge shot into the air. Soon a river
of fudge was flowing down the road.

'Help!' shouted an old lady. She was
stuck in the river of fudge.

Sam quickly pulled his hamster out
of his pocket. 'Wake up, Herc!' said Sam.
'There's work to do.'

Hercules opened one sleepy eye ... and then ran off across the river of fudge. He zoomed faster than the speed of sound. He grabbed the old lady and dragged her out of danger.

'WHEEEE! This is fun!' she cried.

Hercules popped the lady up into a tree.

'What's going on?' asked a passer-by.

'There's trouble at the fudge factory,' said Sam, 'but don't worry! I've got a hamster.'

'Well, he'd better work fast,' said the old lady. 'That river of fudge is heading right for the school!'

'*Yikes*!' cried Sam. 'Herc? What can we do?'

But Hercules was fast asleep again.

Chapter 3

The monster

The river of fudge was nearly at Sam's school. What if Sam and Herc couldn't stop it? Everyone inside would come to a very sticky end.

'Herc! Wake up!' Sam shouted.

Poor Hercules was worn out after rescuing the old lady. If Sam couldn't wake him up, they'd never be able to stop the river of fudge.

Luckily, just then Sam remembered something. He had some superbooster seeds in his pocket. The superbooster seeds would wake Hercules up – fast! He fed Hercules some of the seeds.

'We have to get to the factory and stop that fudge!' Sam shouted.

WHOOSH!

Hercules got Sam to the factory in a supersonic flash.

'Don't go in,' cried a man. 'There's a monster in there!'

But Herc didn't listen to him. He yanked out the window frame and lifted Sam into the factory.

'Good work, Hercules!' said Sam.
They squelched through the thick
oozy fudge inside. The fudge was gushing
out of a big tap. Sam quickly turned it off.

Just then, they saw a
huge, squid-like monster.
The monster was stuffing
its face with fudge.

'Yuck!' said Sam.
'That squid's got very bad
manners. It must be an
alien. It probably got here
in that spaceship we
saw outside.'

Chapter 4

Hercules saves the day

Sam looked down at Herc. He was stuffing his face with fudge, just like the alien.

'Herc, stop that!' cried Sam.

Hercules glanced up with a strange look on his face. The look said: *I want more*!

'Later, Herc,' said Sam.

Suddenly, the alien squid lifted Sam into the air. He was dangling over the monster's mouth.

'Hercules! Help!' cried Sam.

But Hercules was fast asleep again. He slipped out of Sam's pocket ...

... and landed on the alien's head. The alien started to shake. It dropped Sam into the fudge with a splat, and Sam swam to safety.

At once, the alien started scratching itself all over.

'It's covered in spots!' Sam gasped. Hercules was sitting on the monster's head, licking up fudge.

'The alien must be allergic to supersonic hamsters!' cried Sam.

Hercules chased the itchy alien back to its spaceship and ...

WHOOSH

... it was gone.

Chapter 5

What happened to the fudge?

By the time Sam got to school that day, everything was back to normal.

'How did you get rid of the monster?' asked Sam's friends.

'It was all thanks to Hercules, my
supersonic hamster,' said Sam proudly.

'But what happened to all the fudge?'
his friends asked.

Sam shrugged. 'You'll have to ask Hercules,' he said with a grin.

About the authors

Adam and Charlotte met
while teaching on the
Tanzanian island of Zanzibar.
Adam is a storyteller and children's writer.
He spends a lot of time in schools teaching
children and teachers how to become
storytellers and writers. Charlotte worked in
publishing before becoming a non-fiction
author who has written over 100 titles. Now
Adam and Charlotte like to write stories
together because it's more fun that way.

Herc the supersonic hamster is based on a
pet Charlotte had when she was little. Her
hamster was called James and could climb up
the curtains in a flash, but luckily he never
had to fight any aliens.